ENGLISH EROTICISM

ENGLISH EROTICISM

Text by

PIERO LORENZONI

Crescent Books

New York

Acknowledgments

We should like to express our most grateful thanks to Professor Gabriele Mandel, of Milan, who supplied us with a large number of basic documents.

Captions by
Véronique Mercier.

Title-page: "The Happy Huntsman", a work by the great illustrator of the 18th century, Thomas Rowlandson.

Designed and produced by
Productions Liber SA

First English edition published by
Production Liber SA

ISBN 0-517-448033

This edition is published by Crescent Books.
Distributed by Crown Publishers, Inc.

h g f e d c b a

Printed in Italy

An illustration by David Russel for The Canterbury Tales *by Geoffrey Chaucer, the most famous work written during the 14th century.*

FROM ITS ORIGINS TO THE 17th CENTURY

Before the Restoration which reestablished the monarchy, in 1660, erotic works in any form at all were very rare in puritanical England. The first work of this kind, or at least the most famous, in the 14th century marked a parenthesis all the more striking because the King himself distinguished himself in his gallantry. This work was "The Canterbury Tales", by Geoffrey Chaucer (1345-1400), a tale rather like the "Decameron" of Boccaccio, which was characterized especially by the vividness and naturalness of the style. The sovereign on the throne at that time was Edward III, who was responsible for the creation of an order, still today just as prestigious, in circumstances that are worth relating.

One evening the Court was giving a magnificent ball, attended by all the great names of the kingdom and also the ambassadors of foreign countries. The King was there in person, as was his established mistress, the Countess of Salisbury.

This ball would never have had its place in the history of England, had it not been for the fact that the King's favourite *belle* by some misfortune lost one of her garters, which had slid gently right down her leg and fallen on the floor. As the king's courtiers, not knowing what to do in such a situation, stood simply looking at the king to observe his reaction, he, not whitout a certain malicious pleasure, picked the garter up off the floor, turned to them and shouted out, *"Honni soit qui mal y pense"* (Shame be to him who evil thinks). Then, raising aloft the garter under the crystal-clear light of the chandeliers, he added solemnly, "I shall raise it to such a height of glory that even those who mutter and groan this day will be proud to have the honour of wearing it." And immediately, the phlegmatic Edward made good his words, and boldly created the Order of the Garter. The political achievements and the military prowess of this sovereign have long ago been completely forgotten, but not his gallantry, which has earned his mistress's garter the honour of appearing ever since this time on the coat-of arms of England. As for the exclamation proclaimed by the king, this has remained the motto of the order. The libertinage and the sense of eroticism to which this episode bears witness, and "The Canterbury Tales" are nevertheless exceptions that were not to be repeated, or only very rarely, in the centuries that followed.

The rather odd ceremonial pomp, which one might almost describe as obscure, of the reign of Elizabeth I, marks the end of this English Renaissance. Its lack of achievement in the field of plastic arts is compensated for by the splendour of the theatre and poetry, as well as an overflowing *joie de vivre*, the influence and presence of which can still be observed.

Love and death, indissolubly linked, brought a new breathe of life to the Elizabethan theatre, which recalls Greek tragedy; it did not portray its own epoch, but pointed the way along new paths, which are still now far from having all been completely explored. To be convinced of this one need look no further than "A Midsummer Night's Dream" and the erotic declarations of Titania, who says:

Come, sit thee down upon this flow'ry bed,
While I thy amiable cheeks do coy,
And stick musk-roses in thy sleek smooth head,
And kiss thy fair large ears, my gentle joy.

As for the characters Ariel and Corydon, and the "Sonnets", they have kept all their secrets for three centuries: homosexual and Platonic love, the sentimental triangle etc.

Under Cromwell, England became more puritanical than ever and so it was necessary to wait until the time of the return of the monarchy for the realm to experience a period in which gallant, romantic affairs could flourish, along with society scandals and erotic adventures.

Charles II (1640-1685) made no secret, even to the queen herself, of the pleasure that the life of the Court and the women there gave him. In his memoirs, the Earl of Grammont relates that his brother-in-law, Anthony Hamilton wrote on this subject that in the royal palace there reigned an atmosphere of entertainment and pleasure; all the splendour and gallantry that the tastes of a gentle, romantic sovereign could arouse.

Not all the mistresses of Charles II, however, were of noble lineage. It was

CONFESSION   PENANCE

sufficient for the king to meet one of those over-painted, overdressed ladies like Miss Stewart for him to lose his head over her. Grammont speaks especially of Nell Gwyn, who began by selling oranges in London theatres before going on the stage herself. Here she was given a great ovation, as much for her talent as an actress as for her great beauty. The king, on taking her as his mistress, forced her to leave the stage. She then showed herself to be extremely jealous of her rivals, and totally unscrupulous. One day she went as far as to offer some purgative chocolates to a Miss Davis, who had also caught the eye and won the favours of her royal lover; and to make sure that the plan would succeed to the full and bring about the required results, Nell carried it out just before a loving tryst that her victim had granted to Charles II.

Another of the king's mistresses, Lady Castlemayne, was before her marriage called Barbara Villiers, and Miss Stewart, who has already been mentioned, did not hesitate to raise her skirts in front of some members of Parisian high society to prove that her thighs were more beautiful than those of any of her rivals. She was later to become the Duchess of Richmond, since the duke, caught in bed with her by the King, was obliged to marry her and, in doing so, offer her his title.

Writing of the scandalous activities of these two of Charles's favourites, Samuel Pepys, who had formerly been a high official in the Admiralty and had therefore often been at Court, shows very well in his famours *Diary* the laxness of the king's morals and the tolerance of his patient wife faced with the situation:

"By and by, the King and Queen, who looked in this dress, a white laced waistcoat and crimson short petty-coate and her hair dressed *à la négligence,* mighty pretty... Here was also my Lady Castlemayne, rode among the rest of the ladies who the King methought no notice of her; nor when they light did anybody press (as she seemed to expect, and stayed for it) to take her down, but was taken down by her own gentleman... But above all, Mrs Steward in this dress with her hat cocked and red plume, with her sweet eye, little Roman nose, and excellent *Taille,* is now the greatest beauty I ever saw I think in my life; and if ever woman can, doth exceed my Lady Castlemayne, at least in this dresse. Nor do I womder if the King changes, which I verily believe is the reason for his coldness to my Lady Castlemayne".

This freedom in morals was also spread abroad through a certain type of literature, especially in the theatre. This played a more active role still during this period than it had done before the Restoration, since the feminine roles were no longer played, as in the Elizabethan tradition (including Shakespeare) by young men or castrated travestites, but by women or girls, in whose mouths the licentious remarks took on a more pungent force.

If Dryden's plays were lewd, those of Wycherley were almost obscene. More crude, more lascivious still, the comedies of Aphra Behn recall the works of Sappho as much for their delightfully attractive style as for the inclination that the author developed near the end of this life towards homosexuality. But the kind of purity with which he dealt with the question of sex is without precedent in the history of English eroticism, as can be seem by reading the following passage taken from "The Rover or the Banished Cavaliers":

"... I'll be baked with thee between a pair of sheets, and that's the proper still; so I might but strew such roses over me and under me. Fair one, would you would give me leave to gather at your bush this idle mouth; I would go near to make somebody smell of it all the year after". Thus one of the characters addresses a beautiful girl, and a little further on:

"... A nun ! Oh now I love thee for't ! Ther's no sinner like a young saint. Nay, now there's no denying me: the old law had no curse to a woman like dying a maid: witness Jeptha's daughter."

The very height of obscenity, for this period at least, was reached with "Sodom", a play published in Latin in Antwerp in 1684, the author of which signed with his initials E. of R.

"Mentula cum Vulva saepissime jungitur una
Dulcius est Melle, Vulvam tractare Puellae".

Then followed "Sodom or the Quintessence of Debauchery", signed with the same

initials. Even if all the copies in the possession of the printer were destroyed, the two manuscripts, copied several times, have been preserved in numerous librairies, both public and private. The author of "Sodom" is none other than John Wilmot, Earl of Rochester, whose confused sensuality and aggressive, deliberate obscenity Taine emphasizes in his "History of English Literature". A judgment that is certainly not in the least exaggerated, and in no way contradicted by the names Wilmot bestowed on his characters: Fuckadilla, Cunticula, Clitoris, Bolloxinion, Pine, Flux, Cuntigratia, etc., most of them referring in no uncertain manner to a number of sexual practices which were more or less orthodox. One can easily imagine the subject-matter of this five-act play, which takes place in a castle of which all the rooms are decorated with pictures inspired by the famous "positions" of Aretino, representing a wide variety of ways of copulating.

Bolloxinion, the king of Sodom comes forward on the stage and says:

"And so, at the height of my pleasure, I reign, I eat to make love and I make love to eat again;
and with my penis I govern my whole country...

The king allowed himself to be persuaded by Borastus, a specialist in homosexuality, to indulge in sodomy, which he took part in in the company of some forty small boys that the king of Gomorrha had sent to him.

Queen Cuntigratia, for her part, with her ladies-in-waiting, Fuckadilla, Cunticula and Clitoris, give themselves with gay abandon to half a dozen men, as well as to animals of different species. Then follow scenes of incest and copulation in groups. An exchange takes place of *gode-michés* and other actificial phalluses, whose small size rouses the queen's indignation. Those taking part in these orgies become infected with venereal diseases, including gonorrhea and syphillis. To avoid this risk, Bolloxinion reluctantly makes up his mind to go back to "that old tart with the unpleasant vulva", meaning the queen, his wife.

It is thought that Charles II was present at one of the performances of "Sodom", accompanied by several woman, as can be understood from the Prologue:

"I presume that there are no women here to see a comedy such as the one that we are going to play, for it is much too licentious, I am afraid, for the fair sex, and I am quite sure that none will be seen in revealing clothes. Yet there will be certain young ladies here to soothe the heat of their arses! Damned loose women whose cunts are like burning fire ! Now, listen all, and see this play; and be assured that, spurred on by desire before the last of the three acts of this farce has been played out, they will have found the means of making the acquaintance of a fine straight penis; and shamelessly they will guide it towards their arse !"

As for erotic art, unlike the theatre it did not flourish in the England of the 17th century. Drawings, engravings and lewd paintings all came from France which is considered to be the wonderful realm of debauchery. It was not until the revolution of 1688 that the British Isles opened up the way to libertinage. This phenomenon was expressed without any reserve, by means of a number of wanton caricatures in which huge buttocks are maliciously exposed, given up to the power of a clyster.

Among the erotic works imported towards the end of the 17th century was *"L'école des filles"*, attributed to Mililot or Millot. It is a sort of treatise of sexual education, lewd in character, and written on the model of Aretino's "Reasonings", dialogues between two young women. With affected shame, Samuel Pepys wrote in his *Diary:*

"8 Feb. 1668 — Thence away to the Strand to my bookseller's, and there stayed an hour and bought that idle, roguish book, *L'escholle des Filles,* which I have bought in plain binding... because I resolve, as soon as I have read it, to burn it, that it may not stand in the list of books, nor among them, to disgrace them if it should be found."

And again:

"9 Feb. Lord's Day. Up, and at my chamber all the morning and the office, doing business and also reading a little of *L'escholle des Filles,* which is a mighty lewd book, but yet not amiss for a sober man once to read over to inform himself in the villainy of the world... and then they parted and I to my chamber where I did read through *L'escholle des Filles...* and after I had done it, I burned it, that it might not be among my books to my shame."

Although the output of the country itself of erotic novels and comedies was more than sufficient, a great many were also brought in from Latin countries, such as France and Italy: "More attention is given to a short tale by Boccaccio than to a Bible story", wrote Ascham at the time.

And so the 17th century drew to a close in this England in love with the eros, without having been marked by any single original work of great importance, either literary or artistic, which would deserve to have its place in the history of gallantry.

THE EROS IN ENGLAND IN THE 18TH CENTURY

With the arrival of George I on the throne in 1714, women regained some of their power. Gaiety and familiarity formed pleasant ties between the two sexes, without their having any serious consequence. There were never any festivities organized in which there were not a large number of women taking part. Such parties were held entirely for pleasure and soon took on a very intimate nature, favouring the designs of couples, with all the inevitable intrigues, which took the guests away from the main activities of the court and led them to the intimacy of the alcoves at the same time as the courtesans.

Under the reign of George II, from 1727 to 1760, gallantry became more refined; or perhaps rather became a sort of art of intrigue following the rules of a new etiquette. One sought more assiduously the favours of the mistress of an important man than of the Prime Minister, and the high dignitaries of the Church themselves did not feel it beneath them to solicit the attentions of a high-class courtesan. The number of divorces increased rapidly. Covent Garden became the heart of the pleasure-seeking area, whose main attractions were Moll King and the "welcoming houses" of Mrs Stanlope, frequently visited by members of high society; Heatherly, Margeram, Miss Goadby, who only accepted aristocrats and insisted that she be paid in gold pieces. In her luxurious apartments in King's Place, Pall Mall, Charlotte Hayes offered her guests love at a price with virgins who sold themselves for twenty guineas, which was a considerable sum at that time, while a woman of high social rank like Lady Lovett who, "disappointed by her liaison with Lord Alto, hopes to find better", negotiates a price for her charms, the fabulous sum of fifty guineas.

More highly ranked still in this hierarchy of prostitution was Kitty Fisher. She was one of the most famous courtesans in London, and her pretentions were equal to her renown. When the Duke of York left her, he gave her fifty guineas, but she nevertheless gave orders to her servants that he was not to be allowed into her apartments in future. It must be admitted that she found a more generous lover in the person of Lord Montfort. He was so small that one day when Lord Sandwich, whose official mistress she was, arrived on the scene unexpectedly, Kitty succeeded in hiding him under her vast crinoline and then made her way with very short, quick steps into her boudoir, leaving him there without Lord Sandwich having the slightest suspicion of the presence of his rival.

The lax morals and the absence of any taboos at the English Court gave rise to the essentially caricatural eroticism of the greatest illustrator of this type in the 18th century. His name was Thomas Rowlandson. In 1734, the amiable Hogarth composed his

incomparable series of illustrations for "Harlot's Progress". He was a stern moralist and this was his way of drawing attention to the vices and debauchery of a society whose excessive permissiveness he deplored. Florent Feks has pointed out, quite rightly, that the almost bestial faces of his figures, his madmen, unrestrained in their shame and dejection, his murderers cutting up the corpses, his judges with their wild, almost reptilian appearance, express a genre which was to be continued by Daumier and Rouault.

More delicate in his strokes, but much more explicitly erotic, although satirical too, Rowlandson (1756-1827) was born and died in London. His father was quite wealthy, yet finished his life a ruined man, and left his family, who lived in comparative luxury, the

Above, another painting by William Hogarth: "Fashionable Marriage". An aristocrat having caught his wife in the company of a lover has just been stabbed by the lover. The murderer flees through the window.

Right, also by Hogarth, a wood engraving entitled "Cruelty in Perfection". The caption reads:

To lawless Love when once betray'd — Soon Crime to Crime succeeds : — At length beguil'd to Theft, the Maid — By her Beguiler bleeds. — Yet learn, seducing Man ! Nor Night, — With all its sable Cloud, — Can screen the guilty Deed from Sight; — Foul Murder cries aloud.

Very moral ! The fact that one wished to show something about sex had to be carefully concealed. (Turin, Agnelli Collection.)

Here Lieth
the Body

"Before" (left) and "After" (opposite). There exist two different versions of this work. The first shows an interior and the second a setting outside. With a slight touch of irony, Hogarth here shows us a lover begging for the favours of a girl (Before) and the same girl coaxing the lover... as he is exhausted (After).
(Turin, Agnelli Collection.)

responsibility of supporting his son to a substantial extent. Rowlandson began to draw from the age of ten years old, making caricatures of his friends and teachers. He enrolled at the *Académie des Beaux-Arts* in Paris, then continued his studies in London. After having squandered the fortune of his generous family on gambling and women, the painter worked for publishers who were seeking compositions that were particularly erotic, as well as contributing the illustrations for "The History of Tom Jones", published in 1749. The work exposed the licentious, dissolute morals prevalent in England during the 18th century, which were probably the result of a reaction against the despotic power of a puritan moralism. His specifically erotic works are numerous, and a great many of his paintings were, and still remain, in private collections. Pisanus Fraxi, in his "Centuris librorum absconditorum" (1879) enumerates, amongst the best known, more than a hundred and twenty paintings, including "The Rival Knights or the Englishman in Paris", "Inquest of Matrons or Trial for a Rape", *"Les Lunettes"*, based on tales by La Fontaine, "The Harem", "Liberality and Desire", "A Snip in a Rage", "Suzanne and the Very Old Man", etc.

The renown that Rowlandson enjoyed was then so great that the famous painter Reynolds went as far as to compare him to Rubens. His direct successor was George Cruikshank (1792-1878), who was, however, a forerunner of the Victorian style that was to come later, and he was especially interested in fashion, odd and extravagant fashion, women of the period whose exhibitionism and vanity he revelled in exposing.

James Gillray, who preceded him (1757-1815), was an actor before becoming a caricaturist, whose inspiration was also to be found in political satire. Yet, although eroticism is always present, his talent lies in his ability to deform the body and the poses of his characters rather than in beautifying them.

In the erotic art of the 18th century, English artists distinguished themselves by means of a narrative style, which proved to be more lewd than previously.

Above and on all the following pages, engravings by Thomas Rowlandson. This remarkable artist was also a great pleasure-seeker and could always make some observation full of humour and irony suitable to the occasion. He was born in 1756, the son of a financier, and was given a very con-

In chronological order, the first to be mentioned must be "The Toast" (1732), an epic poem in four books, written in Latin by Frederick Scheffer and translated into English by Peregrine O. Donald (volume I). The real author was William King, the son of a clergyman, Peregrine King, and rector of St. Mary's Hall at Oxford.

This work, published in 1732, is a poetic pamphlet attacking Lady Frances Brudenell, the widow of Earl Newburgh, because she had been the cause of the downfall of King's uncle. Wreaking his vengeance by means of his pen, he represents Lady Brundenell by the character of Myra, an old licentious witch, whose debauched character is thus described in not very authentic Latin by William King, for whom, especially, she takes the place of Messalina in the ardour of her devotion to Priapus, the god with his penis always in a state of erection.

ventional upbringing. His works at first met with some success but, when he was about thirty, he gave up his academic style of painting to take up satirical engraving.
Left : "Beauty inclining"; above "A Country Gentleman Freshly Mounted".

"Quos puellulae calore
Nuptae vidit quos furores !
Quae libido, cum vetu-la,
Inflat terra et Mascu-la
Messalina is ceratret,
Messalinam superaret,
Mira, Priapeium decus,
Moechi, Moechae, Moecha, Moechus,

Quid, quod juvenes protervi?
Quos suorum rigent protervi?
Quos suorum rigent nervi?
Tribadum dum Shulickissa,
Venere non intermissa,
Mariuam paptitur, amorum
Haud indocilis novorum..."

But the lust of one single man was not sufficient to satisfy Myra. All the lovers that she could find took advantage of her favours and she still behaved more and more like a nymphomaniac, as can be seen from this extract of a translation of it:

"First a grenadier came forward majestically and allowed fierce feeling to rise up within him, such was his desire to give way to his lust. A confused and burning passion fought violently within his breast. The mighty soldier embraced her and she took measure of all the length of his body and his sexual organ; in the increasingly frantic action that followed, still further accentuated by physical strength and experience, the old witch was like an animal on heat. In chains less harsh than these did Delilah hold her false spouse (...).

"... One evening when I was walking in St. James's Park, it occurred to me that Ranelagh House should still be open, and as I wished to see the place, I took a carriage, alone, without any servant, and set out with the intention of amusing myself until midnight and searching for some beauty who might take my fancy. I was very much impressed by the terrace at Ranelagh, where I had tea served for me, danced a few minuets, without, however, meeting anyone that I knew. I saw several ladies and some very beautiful young women, but I did not have the courage to speak to any of them point-blank.

Annoyed with myself, I decided to leave. It was nearly midnight, and I was going towards the door, hoping to discover my carriage, which I had not paid for, waiting for me. I could not see it anywhere and I stood there feeling very embarrassed. A very pretty woman, who was standing near the door waiting for her carriage, saw my confusion and said to me, in French, that if I lived near White Hall she would willingly take me there in her carriage. I thanked her and, telling here where I was staying, accepted her offer with pleasure. The carriage arrived. A footman opened the door and she got in, leaning on my arm to support herself, then invited me to sit down beside her, telling the coachman to stop in front of my house. I sat down and at once expressed my gratitude to her, told her who I was and added that I was surprised not to have seen her at the last gathering in Soho Square. I was not in London then, she replied. I returned from Bath just today.

I was delighted at my good fortune in having met her, and covered her hands with my kisses. I even dared to give her a kiss on the cheek and, as I met with no resistance on her part, perceiving that, on the contrary she smiled sweetly as she let me do as I wished, I kissed her passionately on the mouth. As she responded with ardour, I became even bolder and without hesitating gave her proof, the most obvious of proofs, of the fire that was burning within me. Flattered by the fact that this seemed not to displease her, so submissive and docile was she, I begged her to tell me where I could meet her again in order to continue my advances and keep her company for as long as I intended to stay in London. She answered:

"We shall certainly see each other again. But be discreet." I swore that I would be, and I did not wish to be toot insistent. Shortly afterwards the carriage drew up, I kissed

Left : "Fumble Cunt" (or "Age does
not bring Wisdom").

Above : "The Unexpected Visit", a
work which appeared in a collection
with the unambiguous title : "Pretty
Little Games for Young Ladies and
Gentlemen with Pictures of good
English Sports and Pastimes".

Left: "Sympathy I".

Right: "The Operation".

Opposite: "College Refreshment".

"The Gallop". A novel kind of horse-riding exploit...

her hands and returned home happy at my good fortune.

I did not see her again for two weeks. At last I met her at the house of a woman. Lady Harrigton had asked me to visit on her behalf in order to present her compliments. This was a certain Lady Betty Germain, an old lady and very illustrious. I was taken into a drawing-room where I was to wait. Then I had the very pleasant surprise of finding there the beautiful woman who had accompanied me home from Ranelagh. She was reading a gazette. I thought of requesting her to introduce me to the mistress of the house. I approached her and asked her if she would be kind enough to grant me this favour. To which she replied very courteously that she was unfortunately unable to do so, since she had not had the honour of making my acquaintance.

"I told you my name, Madam. Do you not recognize me?"

"I recognize you perfectly well, but a moment of madness does not entitle one to recognition."

This reply seemed to me so strange that I let my arms fall to my sides in

"Rural Felicity of Love in a Chaise".

amazement. She calmly went back to reading her gazette and did not address a further word to me during the time we were waiting for the arrival of Lady Germain. Then the beautiful philosopher conversed with her friend for two hours, without giving the least sign of knowing me; speaking all the time with the greatest of courtesy, each time I managed to seize the opportunity of saying a word to her. She was a lady of high rank who enjoyed an excellent reputation in London.

By the middle of the 18th century in London, prostitution had reached the highest society. If the ladies of the nobility satisfied their desires without any thought for their guineas or for their reputation, the girls from the lower ranks sold their charms at certain prices, though they were open to negotiation and some discount could, on occasion, be granted. Catalogues of courtesans were distributed in the capital, with a circulation of thousands of copies. The most sought-after indicated their names, accompanied by a description of their faces, their bodies and their main characteristics; not forgetting their particular talents in sexual matters.

"The Onlooker": *this engraving was inspired by a successful comedy of the time :* The Citizen, *well known to the artist.*

"Promise me to pay them as I pay them", said Lord Pembroke to Casanova, who noted the conversation in his "Memoirs" "and I will give you the lists that will make them come running, here or there, anywhere to your liking".

"Well," answered Casanova, "I prefer to have them here, and I shall give preference to those of them who speak French."

"What a pity! The most beautiful of them only speak English!"

"Never mind! For what I want to do with them, we can manage to make ourselves understood all the same."

"The Inexperienced Yokel".

So Pembroke wrote out several notes in which he noted the prices, which ranged from four to six guineas, except in one case where the price was twelve guineas.

"So this beauty costs double?" I asked him.

"It is not quite like that. But she cuckolds a duke and peer of the realm who supports her and she is only free twice a month.

"Would you do me the honour, my lord, of coming to taste the fruit of my cuckold's skill from time to time?"

"With pleasure but only when the opportunity arises."

"And if you do not manage to find me at home?"

"There is no harm done! I shall go to the inn."

"As I had nothing to do that day", continues Casanova, "I sent my servant to the address of one of those beauties whose price Pembroke had fixed at four guineas, to tell her that I wished to invite her to dine with me. She came but, although I was inclined to think her nice enough, I only found her a good companion to amuse me for a moment after the meal. She certainly did not expect the four guineas, which she had really not earned in my company, but appeared to be pleased when I slipped them into her hand as I saw her out. The second, for the same sum, dined with me the following evening. She was much more beautiful but seemed to me sad and too passive, so that I could not after all bring myself to tell her to undress herself.

On the third day, having given up the idea of making a third attempt by using another of the notes, I went to Covent Garden, where I took my seat opposite a young and very attractive woman. I spoke to her in French and asked her if she would like to dine with me.

"How much will you give me when we reach the dessert?"

"Three guineas."

"Agreed. I am at your disposal."

After the theatre I had a good meal for two served, and she ate with appetite, as I like to see the woman at the table with me do. I then asked her where she lived and was very surprised to realize that she was one of the women that Lord Pembroke had told me would cost six guineas. I came to the conclusion that it was better to manage one's own affairs oneself or at least not to have a high-ranking lord as one's go-between. The other notes offered me women who were not worth wasting time on. The last one, the one who was priced at twelve guineas, pleased me even less than the others... She seemed to me unworthy of such a financial sacrifice and I did not take the opportunity of cuckolding the noble Lord who kept her..."

During this period orgies were no rarity in London. And Casanova describes one in which he took part as the guest of a friend who wished to make him forget the wily intrigues of Miss Charpillon, a girl whose parents had accused him, falsely, of bringing her close to death. So here he was going to the "Canon", a place of ill-fame, where a certain Edgar soon joined him.

"I was counting on your promise," he said to me as he saw me.

"You could not think that I might fail, that I might not keep my word of honour!"

"Such a sentiment reassures me. Your state of melancholy will pass."

"The intelligent, brilliant and kindly conversation of my young friend did much good to my soul in its sadness. And already I felt less cast down when I saw the two delightful creatures who were waiting for us, especially as one of them was French.

"They were really made for pleasure. Nature had abundantly endowed them with

all that could arouse the desires of even the coldest man. I greeted them kindly, but without the enthusiasm that they deserved, and to which, of course, they were accustomed. My somewhat distant and reserved attitude must at first have made them think that I was perhaps a misogynist. I realized this at once and, spurred on by love, I tried to show myself to be more sensitive to their seductive charms. I kissed them passionately but without much joy. I begged Edgar to explain to his compatriot that if I had not been half dead, I would gladly have proved to her, by my acts, that I found her charming. A man who has been three days without either food or sleep cannot hope to be very attentive to the temptations of love. The girls were sorry for me, but words would not have been sufficient to convince them if Edgar had not told them my name. I had such a reputation! When they knew who I was, they treated me with great respect. They and Edgar expressed the wish that Bacchus would goad me on to make love. I let them say this, knowing quite well within myself that their hopes were vain.

"We dined *à l'anglaise*. Which means without the essential part of the meal, the soup. I could only swallow a few oysters, accompanied by a delicious Graves wine. But I felt good and began to enjoy myself as I saw Edgar brilliantly taking charge of the two nymphs.

"At one time, at the height of the gaiety, the young Englishman suggested to this companion that she should dance the "Rompaipe" in all her nakedness. She agreed, on condition that we to should remove our clothes, and that we should find some blind musicians. I said that if it would please them I should be glad to do as they wished, but that, in view of my languorous state, they could not expect me to play the role of the snake, the tempter. They left me free to do as I wished, provided that, if I felt the stirring of desire, I should undress like the others. I promised to do so. An orchestra of blind musicians was called upon and the doors were locked. While the musicians were tuning up their instruments, we all undressed and the orgy began.

"I had before me three magnificent bodies, remarkable for their freshness and their perfect regularity. The music, the lights, the movements, the grace and the gestures of these creatures — all this was extremely seductive. And yet I remained a totally passive onlooker. After having danced a good deal, the young Englishman made the most sensual of advances to the two lovely ladies, passing from one to the other until the exhaustion of his natural forces left him lifeless and obliged him to take his rest. At this point the

Left : "French Dancers at a Morning Rehearsal".

Right : "The Miser". This work has been linked by critics with The Merchant of Venice by Shakespeare. Note the title of the book lying at the old man's feet : L'avarro Deluso.

Below : "The Concert". An old man suffering from gout gives himself up to his two passions at the same time : music and sex !

Left: "The Congregation": Beauty (of the woman) and the height of caricature (the public). Below: "Susanna and the Elders" — a similar theme.

Right, top: "Lonesome Pleasures", or the joys of masturbation, which had been condemned for so long. "The Curious Parson".

Right, bottom: "The Inspection", in the same style.

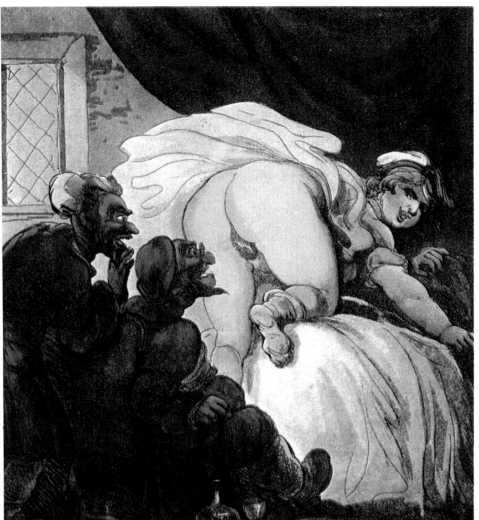

Left, top: "The Star Gazer".
Below: "The Old Husband".

Above: "The Happy Parson" (or
"Stolen Kisses are the Sweetest").
Right: "The Tambourine".

On these pages
and the follow-
ing, further
engravings by the
inexhaustible
Rowlandson.

Left: "Out Posts
of a Camp".

Right: "The
Swings". The
theme of the
swing, used with
erotic intentions,
is to be found in
several different
countries and in
the Far East.
But the engraving
here has, in addi-
tion, a political
implication.

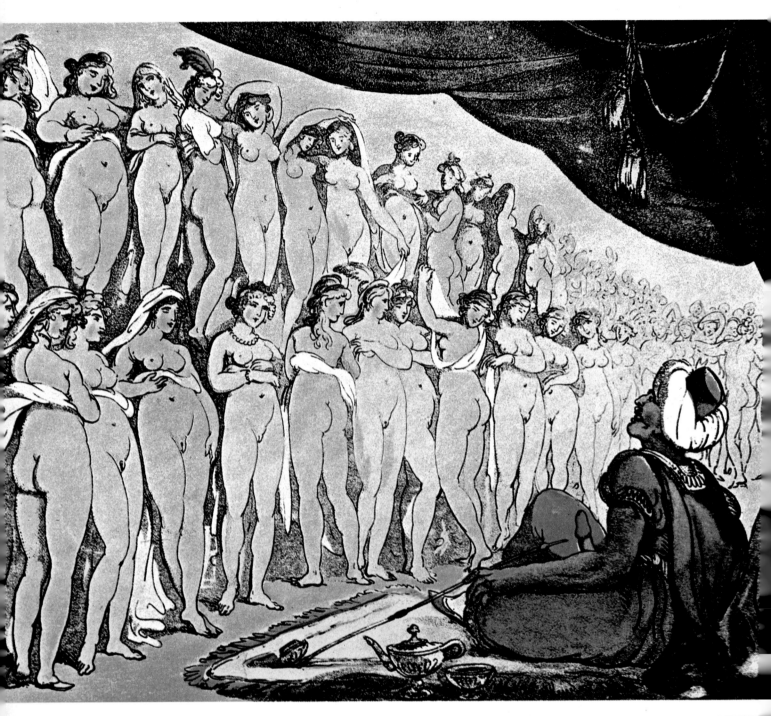

Above : "The Harem".

Opposite : "The Observers".

*Above : "The Pasha".
The East was in fashion
at this time and a
symbol of indecent
assault.*

*Opposite : "The Ride to
Rumford".*

Left: "The Swing". Above: "A Lively Prank".

Frenchwoman came to see if I was showing any signs of life. Realizing my uselessness, she declared me to be infirm. The orgy was over. I asked Edgar to give the Frenchwoman four guineas and to pay the bill, since I had very little money upon my person."

On the subject of prostitution, as a vocation or as a job, reference is often made to Fanny Hill, who came to London from the provinces to seek for an honest situation, but was seduced by the *Beldam* of a brothel who made her sell her body. Fanny Hill is the heroine of the most famous English erotic book.

This work has been the object of numerous translations, and has recently been made into a film. This has earned it worldwide notoriety. The first edition was published in London in 1746. Under the title of "Memoirs of a Woman of Pleasure", its immense popular success soon made way for "The Memories of Fanny Hill", such was the hold that the character had taken on the story.

The author of this earthy novel was John Cleland. He was born in 1709, the son of a

"The Curious Courtesan". This too is a theme dealt with in the erotic art of numerous other countries.

colonel. Having studied at Westminster he became Consul at Smyrna, then in Bombay. He had, however to return to England on account of a trial, and soon found himself in prison for debt. When he finally came out of prison, penniless, he decided to accept the offer made by the publisher Ralph Griffith to pay him a fee of twenty guineas for writing an erotic book. The enthusiastic reception given to it by his readers was such that in a very shorttime Griffith earned ten thousand pounds. This good fortune would hardly have altered Cleland's situation if the Privy Council had not intervened, accusing him of obscenity. When his prosecution was heard, Cleland defended himself, claiming that he had wanted to show the simple folk, despised as they were by the privileged classes, the corruption that existed in certain London society circles. Lord Granville, the Chairman of the Privy Council, not considering that the charges put forward were substantial enough to pronounce sentence on Cleland, merely offered him a pension of one hundred pounds a year until the end of his life... provided that he should give up writing licentious literature for good. Cleland accepted this offer. He was, however, still to write "Memories of a

"Joyous Picking".

Coxcomb" but this was only published a good many years after his death in 1789.

The adventures of Fanny Hill are narrated in a pure, lively style, not in the least slovenly, but using a language that is deliberately pornographic and rich in well-chosen, very pleasant psycho-erotic allusions. Cleland tells the story of the life of a girl of seventeen years old who finds herself in a brothel, loses her virginity there with a young man with whom she is in love, then finds herself alone again after numerous sexual adventures, most of which take place in the brothel to which she is confined.

The young Fanny's first experiences were acquired through one of the women working for "Madame", who had been entrusted with the instruction of the girls of the house. This is how the episode is related:

"Phoebe... was about five and twenty, by her most suspicious account, in which, according to all appearances, she must have sunk at least ten good years: allowance, too, being made for the havoc which a long course of hackneyship and hot waters (to produce an abortion, though Fanny does not say so) must have made of her constitution, and

Top left : "The Discovery". Below :
"Love in the Bath".

Above : "A Hairy Look" or "The
Terror-Stricken Devil".

which had already brought on... that stale stage in which those of her profession are reduced to think of SHOWING company, instead of SEEING it.

"No sooner then was this precious substitute of my mistress's laid down, but she... turned to me, embraced and kiss'd me with great eagerness. This was new, this was odd; but imputing it to nothing but pure kindness... I was determin'd not to be behind-hand with her, and returned her the kiss and embrace, with all the fervour that perfect innocence knew.

"Encouraged by this, her hands became extremely free and wander'd over my whole body, with touches, squeezes, pressures, that rather warm'd and surpriz'd me with their novelty, than they either shock'd or alarm'd me.

"The flattering praises she intermingled with these invasions, contributed also not a little to bribe my passiveness; and knowing no ill, I feared none, especially from one who had prevented all doubt of her womanhood by conducting my hands to a pair of breasts that hung loosely down, in a size and volume that full sufficiently distinguished her sex, to me at least, who had never made any other comparison.

"I lay then all tame and passive as she could wish, whilst her freedom raised no other emotions but those of a strange, and, till then, unfelt pleasure... A lambent fire ran over my whole body, and thaw'd all coldness as they went.

"My breasts, if it is not too bold a figure to call so two hard, firm, rising hillocks... employ'd and amus'd her hands awhile, till, slipping down lower, over a smooth track, she could just feel the soft silky down that had but a few months before put forth and garnishd the mount-pleasant of those parts, and promised to spread a grateful shelter over the seat of the most exquisite sensation, and which had been, till that instant, the seat of the most insensible innocence. Her fingers play'd and strove to twine in the young tendrils of that moss, which nature has contrived at once for use and ornament.

"But, not contented with these outer posts, she now attempts the main spot, and began to twitch, to insinuate, and at length to force an introduction of a finger into the quick itself... that inflamed me beyond the power of modesty to oppose its resistance to

their progress...

"Oh! what a charming creature thou art!... What a happy man will he be that first makes a woman of you!... Oh! that I were a man for your sake!..., with the like broken expressions, interrupted by kisses as fierce and fervent as ever I received from the other sex.

"For my part, I was transported, confused, and out of myself; feelings so new were too much for me. My heated and alarm'd senses were in a tumult that robbed me of all

In the text of this page, the author mentions Fanny Hill. *Modern illustrations of this novel of such renown can be found at the end of the book (p. 92 and following).*

Right: Frontispiece of another erotic novel published in London in 1783 but intended for the French.

liberty of thought; tears of pleasure gush'd from my eyes, and somewhat assuaged the fire that rag'd all over me.

"Phoebe, herself, the hackney'd, thorough-bred Phoebe, to whom all modes and devices of pleasure were known and familiar, found, it seems, in this exercise of her art to break young girls, the gratification of one of those arbitrary tastes, for which there is no accounting. Not that she hated men, or did not even prefer them to her own sex;... but a satiety of enjoyments in the common road, perhaps too, a secret bias, inclined her to make the most of pleasure... now well assured that she had, by her touches, sufficiently inflamed me for her purpose, she roll'd down the bed-cloaths gently, and I saw myself stretched nak'd, my shift being turned up to my neck, whilst I had no power or sense to oppose it. Even my glowing blushes expressed more desire than modesty, whilst the candle, left (to be sure not undesignedly) burning, threw a full light on my whole body.

"No!" says Phoebe, "you must not, my sweet girl, think to hide all these treasures from me. My sight must be feasted as well as my touch... I must devour with my eyes this springing BOSOM... Suffer me to kiss it... I have not seen it enough... Let me kiss it once more... What firm, smooth, white flesh is here! How delicately shaped... Then this delicious down! Oh! let me view the small, dear, tender cleft!... This is too much, I cannot bear it!... I must... I must."

"Here she took my hand, and in a transport carried it where you will easily guess. But what a difference in the state of the same thing!... A spreading thicket of bushy curls marked the full-grown, complete woman. Then the cavity to which she guided my hand easily received it; and as soon as she felt it within her, she moved herself to and fro, with so rapid a friction that I presently withdrew it, wet and clammy, when instantly Phoebe grew more composed, after two or three sighs, and heart-fetched Oh's! and giving me a kiss that seemed to exhale her soul through her lips, she replaced the bed-cloaths over us. What pleasure she had found I will not say; but this I know, that the first sparks of kindling nature, the first ideas of pollution, were caught by me that night; and that the acquaintance and communication with the bad of our own sex, is often as fatal to innocence as all the seductions of the other. But to go on. When Phoebe was restor'd to that calm, which I was far from the enjoyment of myself, she artfully sounded me on all the points necessary to govern the designs of my virtuous mistress on me, and by my answers,

LONDRES

1783

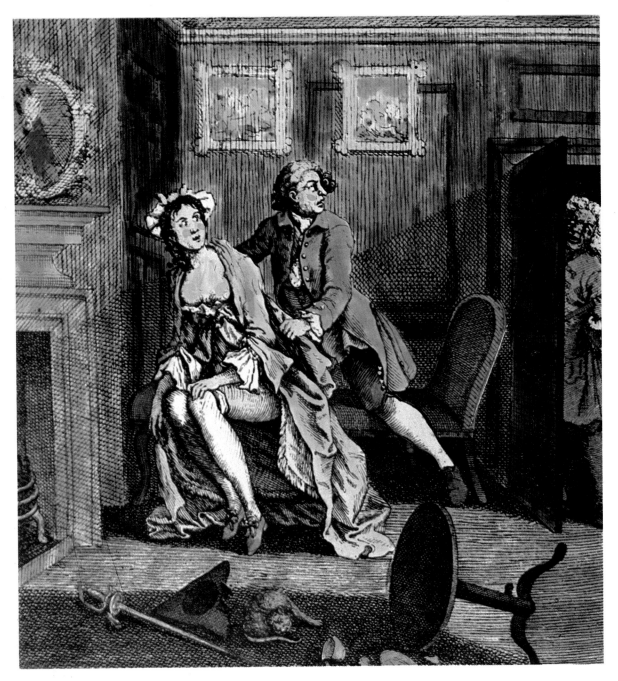

"Inopportune Disturbance": an engraving by A. Tragget for a text presented as a licentious novel "translated from the French", is a lampoon directed at Lord Gloucester(1789). Right: "Captain Hanker and Mrs. Barttelot", an engraving illustrating a work by Joshua Birdtell on... divorce.

drawn from pure undissembled nature, she had no reason but to promise herself all imaginable success, so far as it depended on my ignorance, easiness, and warmth of constitution.

"After a sufficient length of dialogue, my bedfellow left me to rest, and I fell asleep, through pure weariness from the violent emotions I had been led into, when nature (which had been too warmly stir'd and fermented to subside without allaying by some means or other) relieved me by one of those luscious dreams, the transports of which are scarce inferior to those of waking real action.

Captain Hawker and M.ʳˢ Barttelot.

"In the morning I awoke about ten, perfectly gay and refreshed. Phoebe was up before me, and asked me in the kindest manner how I did, how I had rested, and if I was ready for breakfast, carefully, at the same time, avoiding to increase the confusion she saw I was in, at looking her in the face, by any hint of the night's bed scene. I told her if she pleased I would get up, and begin any work she would be pleased to set me about. She smil'd; presently the maid brought in the tea-equipage, and I had just huddled my cloaths on, when in waddled my mistress. I expected no less than to be told of, if not chid for, my late rising, when I was agreeably disappointed by her compliments on my pure and fresh looks. I was a bud of beauty (This was her style), and how vastly all the fine men would admire me! to all which my answers did not, I can assure you, wrong my breeding, they were as simple and silly as they could wish, and, no doubt, flattered them infinitely more than had they proved me enlightened by education and knowledge of the world."

The laxity of morals that prevailed in England in the 18th century was, although very well developed, less so than the laxity enjoyed by France when, in 1798, in the House of Lords, the Bishop of Durham admitted to having corrupted one of his French opponents. A chronicler of the time described the British upper classes like this: "The most popular pleasures of the English, especially of Londoners, are wine, women, dice-playing, in short, a dissolute life. They make no attempt to seek for refinement, at least as far as wine is concerned, nor in the women with whom they associate. As for their courtesans, they like them to drink a lot in order to enjoy to an even greater extent their state of euphoria."

As for the sovereigns of England, their morals were hardly more exemplary.

George III succeeded George II in 1760. His reign was to coincide with a series of important events: the end of the Seven Years' War, the loss of the English colonies in America, the French Revolution, the war against France and the fall of Napoleon. Yet he loved women more than battles, an accusation against him made in this pamphlet:

"Caesar, all-powerful king who brandished the sceptre, was but a pitiful blade; a leg of mutton and his wife were the greatest joys of his life."

ORANGERIE: or — the Dutch Cupid reposing, after the fatigues of Planting. — Vide. The Visions in Hampton Bower.

As for King George IV who, for almost ten years (1810-1819), acted as the Regent, then King, of England until Queen Victoria came to the throne in 1837, he was generally considered to be both immoral and extravagant. Moreover, public opinion reproached him with having taken his own wife Caroline to court simply for the purpose of obtaining a divorce. She is known to have said of her royal husband: "Judge for yourselves the position one finds oneself in when one is married to a man who was dead drunk on the very day of his marriage; a character who spent almost every night of his honeymoon stretched out on the floor, from the moment that he fell there and I left him where he was!"

It is true that the Georges who succeeded each other on the throne of England, humourless in outlook and showing little taste for refinement in their manners and in their sentiments, were not in fact English but originated from Hanover.

The fact is, though, that erotic literature and the erotic arts never had anything but a very limited circulation, apart from a few rare exceptions. It is easily understood, then, that when the subjects of His Gracious Majesty who, for whatever reason it may have been, took some interest in the subject, they welcomed, without any feeling of nostalgia, the arrival of the 19th century.

*The theme of the engraving above is:
"The Empress of Russia Receiving
Her Brave Guards". It is attributed
to Johann Heinrich Ramberg, but
others believe it to be by Rowlandson.*

"Spanner".

Designd & Etchd by R Newton 1795.

London Publ

TOO MUCH or ONE THING GOOD FOR NOTHING.

On these pages, three works by R. Newton. Above: "Too much of one thing good for nothing".

Right, top: "How the country parson takes an interest in the affairs of his flock".

Opposite: "After Duty". These clergymen are accused of practising what they prohibit.

R. NEWTON

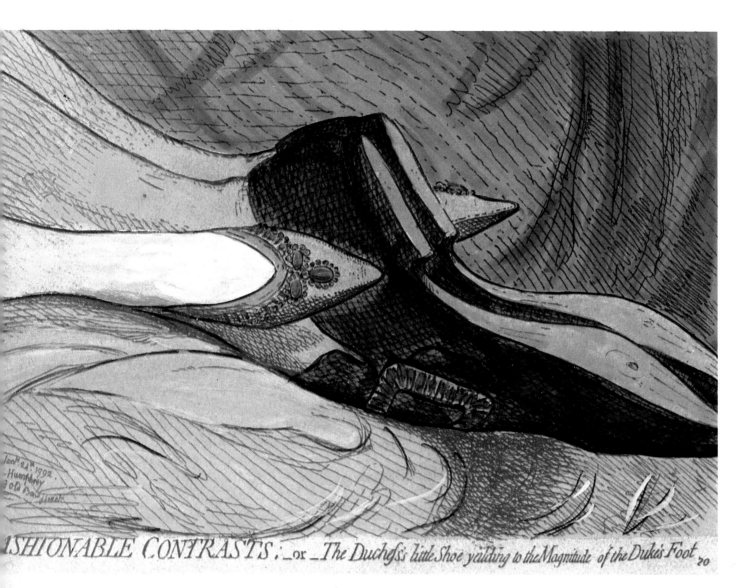

FASHIONABLE CONTRASTS: _ or _ The Duchess's little Shoe yielding to the Magnitude of the Duke's Foot.

Above : "Fashionable Contrasts or The Duchess' Shoe yielding to the Magnitude of the Duke's Foot", a caricature by Gillray, 1792.

Opposite : "The Earl of Rochester", an illustration for an autobiography recalling one of the Earl's amazing adventures

Right : Frontispiece for another autobiographical novel, "The Ups and Downs of Existence", by Edward Sellon.

THE ENGLISH EROS IN THE 19th CENTURY

It is well known that the attraction of what is forbidden is one of the most powerful stimulants of the eros. Making pornography even slightly more accessible is really a means of restraining it, while seeking to repress it is probably the best way of making it prosper, by increasing its importance even more, thanks to its clandestinity.

It is not surprising then to realize just how successful erotic literature and art were with the British at a time when Queen Victoria went as far as to order that covers should be put on table and piano legs, which might give rise to lascivious thoughts.

The result was not long in making itself felt. Publishing erotic works became a flourishing industry. The titles of books published from 1820 to the end of the century certainly leave no room for doubt about the kind of subject treated and distributed secretly.

A handbook intended, so we are told, for young women, called "The Bedfellows" introduces us to the intimite relations of those sharing the bed in question, and "The Adventures, Intrigues and Amours of a Lady's Maid" reveals the secrets of a great lady's servant. "The Modern Rake" relates the exploits of a modern libertine, while "Scenes in the Seraglio" initiates us into the mysteries of a harem, as does also "The Lustful Turk".

Of a slightly more intimate nature, there were also books giving practical advice to neophytes wishing to learn: "How to Make Love", followed by a work which aimed at teaching them... the way of giving birth. Nor must we forget the life and secret correspondence of two young ladies who, being "cousins and very beautiful", are about to reveal, so we are told, their first sexual feelings "in the minutest detail", as well as "the delightful pleasure of enchanting dreams of love". "Magnificent engravings" illustrated these publications which, it seems, met with great success when they appeared in the 1820s, then again twenty years later, in the name of the "Society of Vice", and yet again after 1860 through the master pornographer, William Dugdale.

To this list, which is by no means exhaustive, must however be added: a "Festival of Love, or Revels at the Fount of Venus", where the fount of Venus is the scene for orgies; "The Romance of Lust", which glorifies debauchery and appeared in 1879, and, the same year, "The Pearl", which will be mentioned later. In 1880, great interest was taken in

"The Story of Dildos" which deals with artificial penises. Then in the following year came the publication of "The Loves of Venus, confessions of a Young Bride". Six years then passed before the appearance of "The Autobiography of a Flea", the woman narrator of which imagines herself to be a flea... And then colonial eroticism made its entrance in 1889, with "Venus in India, or Love Adventures in Hindustan"! But this Indian Venus soon has a rival in the person of "Flossie", a bewitching beauty of fifteen years old, whose passions were revealed, in 1897, "by one of those who worshipped at the temple of this young goddess". And the doors of the 20th century opened slightly at last with "A Night in a Moorish Harem", a new version, very un-Victorian, or the "Thousand and One Nights", in Moorish fashion.

Then came the invention of photography, which brought about radical changes and caused the print to die out. The daguerrotype became the first of the "mass media" of erotic art. In his "Index librorum prohibitorum", published in 1877, Pisanus Fraxi (Henry Spencer Ashbee) relates that in the studios of Henry Hayler, a photographer who was famous throughout Europe, the police seized no less than 130,248 obscene negatives and 5,000 plates, which were promptly destroyed. Hayler himself had to go into hiding to avoid being put in prison. Certain newspapers of the time, "The Daily Telegraph" and "The Times", asserted that in the most suggestive of these photographs one could distinguish the features of the master himself, his wife and his two sons.

But the two subjects which predominated in the domain of the English eros, from the end of the 18th century right up to the first half of our own century, were flagellation and the deflowering of virgins; two themes which were to distinguish British eroticism from that of all other countries.

Some people consider that the phlegmatic nature which seems to be characteristic of the English concealed at that time a mixture of pride, aggressivity and violence, which revealed itself more than ever before during the 19th century, in the wake of an imperialism which, with its vast and widely-scattered colonies, controlled almost a quarter of the planet. The number and the condition of the peoples who had submitted to the British, starting with the Indians, could not but encourage the British, it seems, to act in a haughty and arrogant manner, and for the most part to manifest a certain complex of superiority. Another reason for this attitude lay in the excessive severity of the English colleges and schools, where the whip was the rule, and the teachers were authorized by the parents to make regular use of corporal punishment to chastize pupils who had just committed some minor disciplinary offence.

One of the first books published in England on flagellation, "the English vice", as it is justifiably called, had appeared as early as 1780 under the very explicit title of "The Birchen Bouquet". The work was presented as a collection of "curious and original" anecdotes, whose heroine delighted in administering strokes of the whip. There followed in 1788, "Venus, School-Mistress of Birchen Sports" in which the tradition of corporal punishment in schools appears as a sporting activity this time, with no other purpose but sexual pleasure, under the direction of a Venus promoted to the rank of schoolmistress.

Of the hundred or so volumes produced in England during the 19th century on the subject of flagellation as a means of obtaining pleasure, the "Experimental Discourse"

Above : "Flagellation", an anonymous illustration for an English version of the works of the Marquis de Sade, 18th century. Right : "The Pleasure of Flagellation or : When the Queen punishes her Subjects in order to Punish Herself", a satire attributed to Ramberg. Below : Frontispiece for the book The Exhibition of Female Flagellation, *published in London by William Dugdale in 1860.*

(1836), the work of a certain Colonel Spanker, perhaps deserves special mention. The author advocates this form of chastisement which he credits with definite social and psychological advantages. He speaks of the exciting sexual and sensual pleasure that one can experience, in his opinion, by tyrannizing and humiliating a beautiful, respectable young woman. The Colonel expressed his views in this way at a meeting of the Society of Aristocratic Flagellants in the elegant area of London known as Mayfair; and the text of what he said was immediately reproduced in a privately-circulated brochure.

The speech, intended for an "elite" of flagellants who took their pleasure in torture

carried to its extreme limits, opened thus:

The experimental discourse, as its title indicates, deals with the state of ecstasy which can come, in fact, from the pleasure obtained by means of cruelty, both physical and moral.

The very heights of enjoyment can only result from two factors: first, from the fact of imagining that the object of our desires approaches our ideal of beauty: or, secondly, when this object inspires in us sensations of a most violent nature. No feeling is as strong as pain; and its effects are as real as they are unquestionable. Pain cannot deceive, unlike the farce of eternal pleasures at acting which women excel, but which rarely corresponds to the truth. The man who is capable of producing the most violent of impressions on a woman and can succeed in disturbing and agitating the female organism until it reaches the point of paroxysm will achieve himself the very heights of sexual pleasure.

These observations constitute the quintessence of the philosophy expounded and supported by Sade; but the author of this book is also concerned with showing the extent of physical pleasure produced by the refinements in the field of torture to which his selected victims have to submit.

Basing his ideas on this theory, Colonel Spanker discovers a young lady well-known in his circle, Julia Ponsonby, a delightful blonde of seventeen years old, whose mother, a widow, herself obliged to go abroad for a while, was looking for a respectable lady to whom she could entrust her daughter during her absence.

Thus began a series of sessions of flagellation, which were the source of great stimulation and pleasure for the colonel and his acolytes, the members of the "Society of Aristocratic Flagellants", which he had founded himself. A notable feature of the society: the group numbered a dozen women, amongst the most attractive and the most frequently-seen in the best circles in London, some of whom were known to be very cruel.

Less aggressive than Spanker's friends were "The Merry Order of St. Bridget", amongst whom the whip took pride of place in many different ways, given in detail by Margaret Anson in a book that her friends published at their own expense in 1857. In it the author describes her own initiation into the rules of this exclusively female coterie:

"Take off your coat!" said a voice that I recognized as being that of Mrs. D..., an English lady, rather stout and fat, about forty years of age, full of life and malice.

"Now, follow me!"

Another illustration from Country Retirement. *This plate shows a notice with a curious inscription : "She Romps Club, Rules 1753".*

The door opened and I was shown in. Then the door closed behind me... and was bolted. I heard around me the sound of stifled laughter and a voice from the back cried out:

"Silence, ladies, if you please !"

Someone tapped sharply three times on the table and the same voice asked: "Who is this young lady?"

Instructed by Mrs. B..., I replied, as I had been told to do:

"A candidate hoping to become a member of the Merry Order of St. Bridget."

"Are you ready to serve the Order to the best of your ability and to help, in any way your mistress asks you, in the performance of the ceremonies of the Order?"

"Yes, I am!"

"Do you solemnly undertake never to speak of what you might see, hear or do inside this room, under penalty of losing your title!"

"Yes, I promise!"

"Do you know the aims of the Order?"

"Yes, I do."

"What are they?"

I replied according to the instructions that I had received.

"Salutary and agreeable flagellation by means of birches reciprocally used by members in the course of their gatherings."

"Have you ever been whipped?"

"Of course I have."

"Do you promise to submit yourself to this flagellation that the "Merry Order" will inflict on you without rebelling or protesting?"

"I do."

"Then let us prepare her."

I heard more stifled laughter and realized that Mrs. D... was shaking with restrained amusement as she carried out her orders; she removed my dressing gown. She lifted my petticoats and my chemise up to my shoulders so that I could show my round, fleshy, milk-white buttocks. At the same moment a terrible stroke with the birch fell upon my posterior, followed by a rapid succession of other strokes. I wept and struggled but, deep inside me, I found more pleasure than suffering in the experience.

At last, after a new series of fierce blows, I was made to kneel down, and Mrs. B... gave me a birch and told me that I had now become a slave of the "Merry Order of St. Bridget" and that I was authorized to take part in their ceremony..."

If birches and whips appear in a large number of the novels that extol the sufferings and pleasures of flagellation carried out with leather straps, or simply by means of a slap, though administered with extreme violence, the instrument of chastisement which was the most appreciated by flagellants was at that time the "Berkley Horse". This was a sort of articulated ladder, adjustable at will, with an opening for the head and the external sexual organs of the patient, who was firmly tied up with ropes and chains... The usual price was fixed at one pound for the first drop of blood which spurted from the flesh of the voluntary martyr; and as much as five pounds for the inestimable consolation of losing consciousness!

The "Berkley Horse" owed its name to Theresa Berkley who invented it in 1828. Theresa ran a brothel at 28 Charlotte Street, Portland Place. She was expert in the art of whipping, desirous of satisfying the most difficult of clients and, at the same time, an excellent business-woman. She is thought also to have edited a book entitled, "The Favourite of Venus", in which she revealed "the secrets of the life of a devotee of pleasure" (taken from the intimate jottings of her diary) and which begins with this exclamation:

"Oh Heavens! What a sensation I am enjoying! How could I ever describe the pleasures of the whip? Its magic enchantment is so intoxicating, so fascinating!..."

More spicy and more discreetly erotic is another novel, amongst the most famous, "Curiosities of Flagellation", which tells of events and facts collected by an amateur. Of this work, which first appeared in 1875, only two of the five volumes initially announced were, in fact, printed: "The Jeweller's Housekeepr" and "Mrs. North's School".

"The Jeweller's Housekeeper" is a long tale which, unlike the other English works of the same kind written during the 19th century, presents flagellation as a practical aphrodisiac, that is, as an end in itself, if not more. In other words, the author, who is anonymous, tries to persuade his readers that the victims of the whip experience, in spite of everything, a pleasant, sexually-satisfying sensation, as much, if not more, than those performing the act.

The heroines, the daughters of the jeweller Warren, Alice who is fourteen, and Annie, two years older, are "two of the nicest persons in the area of Highgate". Their

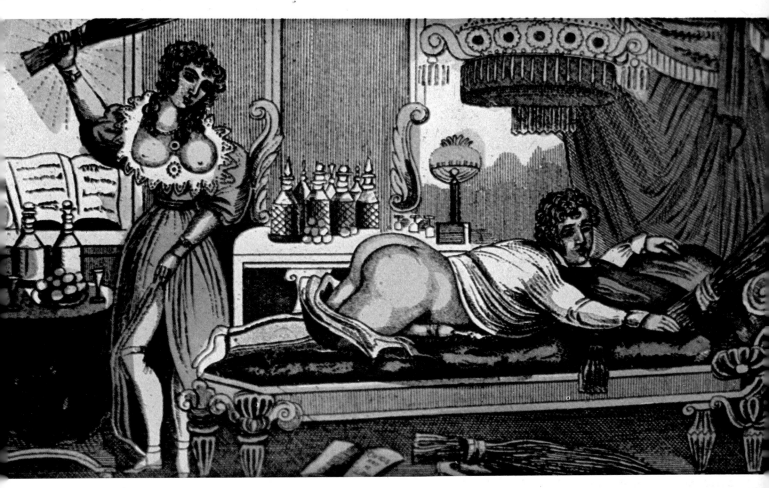

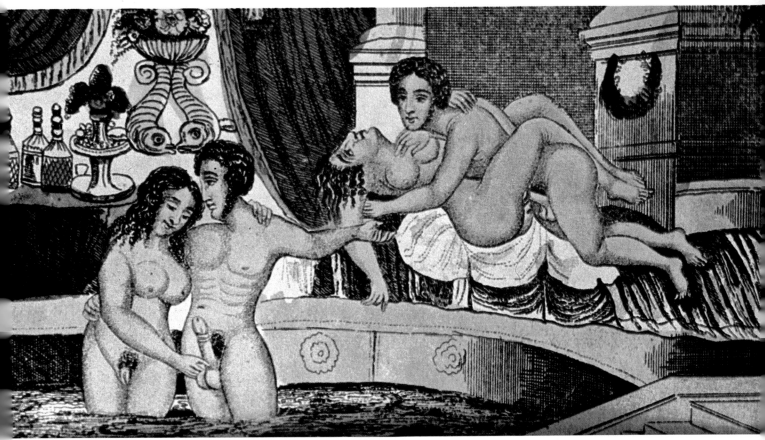

father, who lives in the heart of London, gives himself up to rousing the sexual excitement that is within him by whipping, or in watching Alice and Annie carry out the whipping. When he is not doing it himself, he entrusts them for this purpose to a dominating housekeeper. Brought half-naked to her bed, after having been beaten by her father, Annie confesses to her sister that she has experienced a delightful sensual pleasure and that she has reached the heights of a most perfect ecstasy. At this moment, Alice is preparing to massage the illtreated posterior after she has removed the dress:

"... her spread thighs allowed a glimpse of the seductive little lips of her tiny virginal vulva, and Alice brushed her hand over her mons Veneris to soothe the burning sensation of this so delicate spot. Annie, delighted, put on her nightdress, rapidly performed her toilet for the night, blew out the candle and cast herself down upon the bed. Their lips met in a voluptuously loving kiss.

"Annie, dear," said the younger of the sisters, "lie down on me, your stomach close to mine", and speaking thus to her, she slid her hand gently towards the most secret parts of her sister's body. "Oh! how your burn! Put your most private parts against mine to warm your little sister!" sighed Alice.

"Oh! Alice, how well you caress me, oh, oh, touch me there," cried Annie. "But let us speak softly; the devil might hear us and carry us away."

"It's beyond belief", moaned the younger sister with pleasure. "It's beyond belief how you excite me when you move upon me, and sit astride me like a wonderful jockey!"

The elder sister answered her:

"I have no longer any fear of the whip, you know. In fact it makes me experience a heavenly warmth. Alice, my love, touch me with your fairylike fingers. Oh! oh! oh! kiss me, love me, oh!... I feel that I am all clammy and that your hand is too, my treasure, what delight!..."

Amongst the instruments of pleasure or erotic torture works of the Victorian age mention the artificial phallus and other *gode-miché* ("dildo" in English), rarely touched upon by English authors, unlike their French counterparts of last century, whose female characters frequently made use of them to console themselves in the absence of their male partner. A mischievous tribute was paid to them, moreover, in one of the serialized novels published by "The Pearl", a monthly magazine intended to convert its readers to "voluptuous and facetious reading", produced at Oxford by the University Press in 1879. This was one of the most obscene of British publications, and enjoyed privileges such as no

other periodical of this or any other type had been granted since the 18th century.

It was also "The Pearl" that narrated the adventures of Lady Pockingham, the subtitle of which, "They all do it", leaves very little doubt as to the object of her activities. Here is an extract from it:

"Well then, what is the programme?" Alice asked Lady Bertha.

"Sainte-Aldegonde and Montairy are saving themselves for tomorrow's important ceremony", she answered. "What weak things men are! As if we should want to save ourselves! Victoria and I never have enough of it; the more we have the more we want; and the less able they are to satisfy us. And speaking of women's rights, they ought to oblige their husbands to find a replacement of some sort when they cannot assuage our desires".

"Well! If you have a pair of good dildos, Beatrice and I will try to satisfy you a little while dear Corisande helps us with a beautiful birch", answered Alice.

The dildos that were brought were of monstrous size: they were made of very fine vulcanized rubber; well moulded and beautifully finished, with all their accessories; we tied them together after having spread them with a cream made of milk and gelatine. We were all completely naked.

Lady Bertha took me on her knee; she kissed me lasciviously and manipulated the artificial penis as if it had been a living one.

"What a fine boy!" she said laughing, "but it is not too big for me!".

At the same time I busied my fingers with touching and caressing her clitoris. Her lips clung to mine, as if she would draw my soul out of me, roused as she was by the gentle stroking of my hand, which had brought about the erection of her well-developed clitoris. She led me to a couch and I introduced the artificial penis into her: her pelvis responded to each thrust, while I felt the smarting blows of the birch that Corisande was administering to Alice and myself in turn; how delightful it was! I responded with all my burning ardour to the loving caresses of Lady Bertha, who held me firmly by the buttocks while she managed with two fingers of her right hand to titillate my arse and my clitoris at the same time. Alice and her companion were quickly forgotten; I think that I have never experienced anything so delightful in the whole of my life. The combination of all these sensations drove me mad. The beautiful creature who writhed about in ectasy under my body; our lascivious kisses, the heat and the charming caresses on my two orifices brought me to such a state of ecstasy that when I thrust the penis backwards and forwards inside

MOSES, erecting the Brazen Serpent in the Desert

MOSES in the Bulrushes!!

her, it seemed to me to melt into a sea of lubricity.

After a moment, I asked her if I could play the part of the man and if she would let me touch her swollen clitoris, as I was certain to feel great pleasure in the act. "Certainly, darling", she said, "I often do this with Victoria; remove the artificial penis". As quickly as possible we changed places and I begged her to place herself in front of my mouth so that I could kiss her private parts and caress her clitoris, which caused me such excitement.

And so it was done and I had a magnificent view of all the garden of love. A splendid mound covered with shining black hairs, the bright pink irregular lips of her sweet sexual organs, just slightly open, from which projected over a length of almost four inches a swollen, fleshy clitoris, almost as fat as the thumb of a man.

I opened the lips with my fingers, lasciviously ran my tongue over the most sensitive parts, then took this glorious clitoris in my mouth, twisting my tongue around it and nibbling at it with gentle bites. It was too much for her; she cried out:

"Oh! oh! you are making me come, darling!" And she released her fluid in profusion, so that it burst out into my mouth and ran down my chin."

In Victorian England, erotic literature and feminine fashion did not advance together hand in hand. In the first half of the 19th century, elegant ladies had nothing, if one may be so bold as to say so, between their legs; their underclothing hardly came down below their hips. Then, worn beneath the crinoline, the pantaloon had its followers in high society, while others inclined rather towards "drawers".

Soon, great ladies like the Duchess of Bedford or Lady Charlotte Lindsey favoured the pantaloon and showed them off even in the streets of the City. On the beach or at the baths, it was essential. Its use remained the privilege of wealthy women but the most sophisticated of them and the most discreet, remained faithful to drawers, which had no effect on the bulkiness of their dresses and had the advantage of being invisible.

In 1851, Amelia Bloomer, a militant American feminist arrived in England. Under her dress, which was relatively short, she was clad in a baggy pantaloon, caught in at the ankles, that was from then on to be called a "bloomer". On the continent, the so-called "Turkish" pantaloon was in fashion, of identical cut and generally sported under a tunic of red and black silk which came down to just below the knee. The bloomer fashion was only a limited success, since this odd garment attracted too much attention from curious bystanders, which was not to the taste of everyone. Many elegant women gave up very quickly what was considered at the time to be a brazen adherence to fashion. It was,

Above and below : two illustrations which appeared in the monthly The Pearl, *published in Oxford (1879) : "The Complex Position" and "The Life of the Blacks".*

Right : "The Busy Night", a sheet on the subject of love dating from 1888.

THE BUSY NIGHT.

No 1.

A lady once on going to bed
Felt something on her knee.
Taking a light, she raised her dress
And found it was a flea.

No 2.

She said her prayers, retired to rest,
And slumbe sweet did she
Until she woke all over bumps
Inflicted by that flea.

No 3

She scratched with force. and murmered low.
"There is no rest for me,"
Then lept from bed in light attire
To catch the horrid flea.

No 4.

She hunted high she hunted low,
But nowhere could she see
That playful midnight enemy,
That vile tormenting flea.

No. 5

The damsel had another look
Then murmered, Oh! dear me
How can I sleep until I catch
That tantalising Flea.

No 6.

She searched the bed. she searched the clothes.
"Wherever can it be,"
At last she pounced upon the foe,
This little lively flea.

No 7

She grasped it in her lily hand,
And cried ' I'll settle thee.
I'll put YOUR light out in this THIS light
You aggravating flea.

No 8.

Within the candle fat she placed
That insect with much glee,
And as it gave a dying kick
Said "Bon Soir, Monsieur Flea."

No 9.

At last she dropped off sound to sleep,
And all I want's "One D."
For this authentic history of
"The Lady and the Flea."

however, very successful with girls and blossoming young women of high society, on both sides of the Channel, as can be seen from the engravings used as illustrations in numerous novels of children's literature.

Quite different are the characters of Aubrey Beardsley (1871-1898). Here one sees women wearing bloomers, vast and complicated corsets, close-fitting dresses in some dark colour, relieved by something brighter too, as well as men, completely naked, whose sexual organ has been brought into full view by the most famous master of eroticism of Victorian days. His works are a subtle combination of the refinements of a decadent style, carried out by means of a light stroke, elegant and sinuous, which knew how to depict the sensuous and secret contours of a thigh and express the exaltation with which this cult of Priapus, the rustic god with the constantly erect penis, inspired him. He sketched with the same careful attention to detail the fall of the material of his subjects' clothing and the lightness of muslin. An enthusiastic disciple of Oscar Wilde, whose homosexual relationships, notably with the son of Lord Douglas, earned him two years' imprisonment and the condemnation of the whole of puritanical England, Beardsley was also the illustrator, acclaimed by some but scorned by others, of the author of "Salome", and of "Lysistrata" by Aristophanes. In addition he had the task of acting as artistic director of the publication known as "The Yellow Book", today almost impossible to find.

The subjects of Her Majesty Queen Victoria rated highly not only flagellation, which has already been discussed at length above, but also the pleasure of deflowering very young girls with no experience. Amongst the vast number of novels dealing with this subject, sometimes with a somewhat morbid sense of humour, one of the most often quoted is "My Secret Life". The revelation of this secret life is owed, it is thought, to two eminent masters of erotic literature, George Legman and Sir Henry Spencer Ashbee (Pisanus Fraxi). This is without doubt the longest of its kind ever published, since it contains no less than 4,209 pages!

"My Secret Life" is presented as a collection of autobiographical memoirs told by an Englishman who, in the manner of Don Juan, shamelessly draws up the incredibly long list of women, young or more mature, atduscreettractive or rather plain, respectable or corrupt, with whom he has had sexual relations some time during the course of his life. This work has proved to be the most important documentation on one otherwise little-known aspect of British society in the 19th century. As Steven Marcus very rightly remarks in his book, "The Other Victorians", precious information is to be found here about the morals and customs of the period, and especially about the way in which "forbidden pleasures" were codified at that time and, one might almost say, institutionalized.

For example, if anyone wanted to meet a prostitute, or some other lady rather more

concerned about her reputation, he had a great many discreet places where the sexual act could be performed. The author (or the man who claims to be the author) of "My Secret Life" speaks from experience. Welcoming rooms are in no short supply. Thus a notice with *Beds* printed on it hanging in the window of a café left prospective customers in no doubt of their welcome.

Suffice it to say that morality left much to be desired about 1850, even if the apocryphal "memoirs" of "My Secret Life" were probably written some time between 1870 and 1880. Virginity was far from being always regarded as a treasure worthy of being fiercely defended, even in the case of the least worldly-wise young women.

"I undressed to the point of being simply in my shirt", relates the hero of "My Secret Life", "While she took all her clothes off and stood naked; then she threw herself on the bed, though I had not asked her to do so. It had never happened to me before to see a young woman in the grip of a cold, deliberate desire to be deflowered..."

"... I clasped the girl closely to me; her vagina was just at the height of my testicles. I felt completely calm and cold, because my sperm was not yet driving me into action. More than anything, I wanted to deflower her and I felt no desire to ejaculate. Above all I wanted to possess her and the sudden thought came to me that I needed to hurt her.

"Come closer to me, my little one", I said to her and she immediately obeyed me.

I raised her legs in such a way that her ankles should be against my chest and her thighs against my naked stomach; once again I touched my penis, which, although small, was still rigid; then, holding her thighs in a raised position, I put my penis between the lips of her little vagina, which I had moistened with saliva, and began to thrust. The more I thrust, the more her light little body moved forward on the bed.

"Keep your legs well up, my treasure", I murmured to her.

Frantically I clasped her even closer to me. She helped me by pushing her buttocks forward, my penis still being inserted between the large lips, and harder than ever.

Then, thrusting more strongly, I penetrated her as quickly as possible; she closed her eyes and her mouth was slightly open as she panted a little; I saw her teeth clenched firmly together.

"Oh..haoho.." she moaned through her clenched teeth.

"Am I hurting you?"

"Only a little", replied the courageous girl, in a mere whisper.

I thrust again. I felt that my penis had met an obstacle; something soft, which acted as a separation and enveloped my organ and which stretched as I thrust; and suddenly I realized that it had happened. I thrust again.

"Oho...aha,ahao", she groaned with a little shudder.

Immediately my penis found itself at ease and felt comfortably installed in the vagina in which I was continuing to thrust.

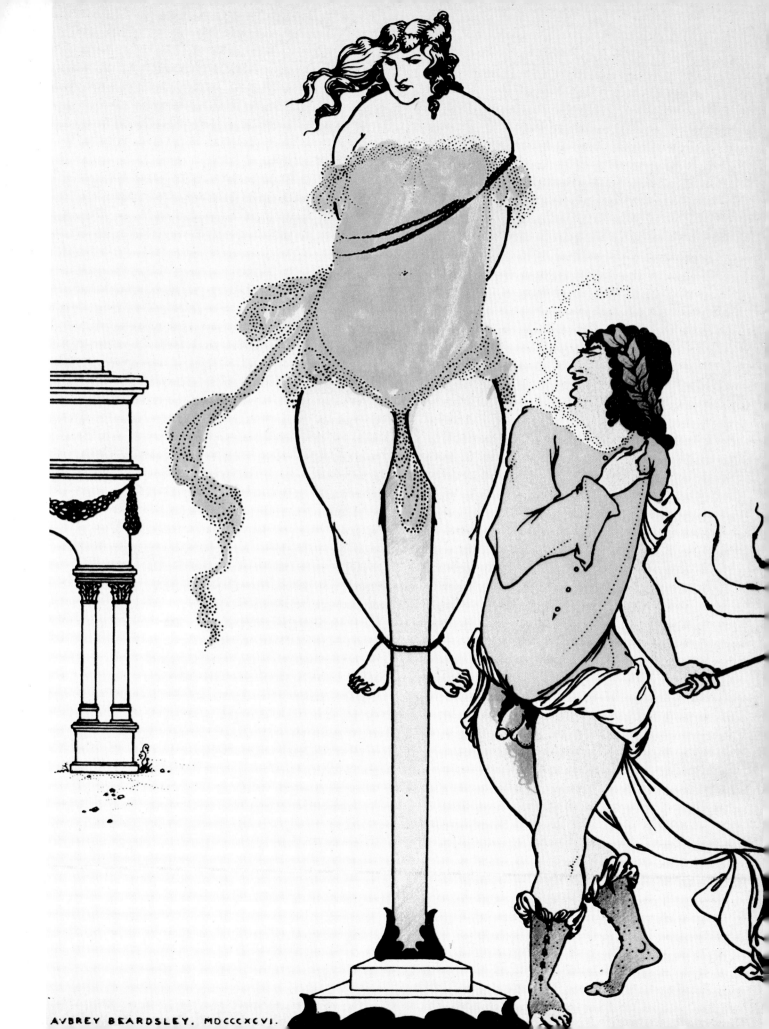

AVBREY BEARDSLEY. MDCCCXCVI.

AVBREY
BEARDSLEY.

ERDA

A *further three drawings by Beardsley, produced two years before his death at an early age : "The Toilet of Lampito", "Erda" and, right, "Bathyllus posturing", an illustration for Juvenal's Satires.*

"I am inside", I cried, letting my hand stray at once between her thighs and examining the base of my penis which was resting against the vagina of the girl, while my testicles covered the crack in her buttocks. Her virginity had been overcome. Oh! The proud pleasure of that moment, while I remained still, savouring the delightful sensation produced by the rubbing of my organ against the walls of her vagina. There could be no mistake about it: I had penetrated deep into this narrow slit which, a few moments earlier, hardly seemed capable of opening wide enough to receive even my finger..." If the leading character in this scene was more than willing and expected no reward in exchange for her virginity, a good many others, hardly out of childhood, were obliged to sell theirs, and at a high price, pushed into it by their own parents or by go-betweens based in the poor quarters of town, but also in the most exclusive areas of London.

In 1885, the "Pall Mall Gazette" published a series of articles, whose contents immediately aroused a real storm of protestation throughout England. The copies of this paper were seized everywhere. A great many vendors, caught selling them, were arrested on the spot and the headquarters of the "Pall Mall Gazette" was taken by storm. There followed an avalanche of anonymous letters, accusations and protestations by senior officials, personalities of high rank and well-known businessmen. Anybody who was anybody in London (males, of course) exploded in wrath with incredible violence. In the House of Commons, Members put down questions for thegovernment asking for the arrest of the journalists concerned. But why was there such a fierce reaction? Simply because some of the "Gazette" staff had carried out a detailed enquiry amongst brothelkeepers who ran their houses in more or less strict clandestinity, amongst pimps and also their young victims.

Then there came to light the hidden corruption behind the front of puritan morality, which was one of the pillars of Victorian society. The strictness, the harsh, prudish inflexibility were nothing but a hypocritical facade supported by haughty pride and scorn. Politics could not be kept out of the scandal; the responsibility was quite naturally put on France, who was openly criticized as the seat of all perversion.

In accordance with the law of the time, an English girl who had reached her thirteenth birthday was considered to be a mature woman and, as such, had the right to dispose of her body to anyone she wished. Yet the "Pall Mall Gazette" enquiry showed that at least 80% of the poor, naive girls in London lost their virginity for a price somewhere between 5 and 20 pounds. And even worse, the police connived at this and were protected by very high-ranking personalities belonging to the world of finance, or even Members of Parliament! Understandably so; since it was they who, in the brothels run by "mistresses of vice", took advantage of the rare and refined pleasure offered by the plucking of the budding flower of the still under-age boarders.

"The man was beside me, with nothing on", relates one of the girls who was indecently assaulted by a Member of Parliament, "and I began to scream and begged him

to go away. He took no notice, but pulled out a huge hard thing, raised my skirt and pushed it into my little orifice. He hurt me so much, so terribly badly, that I tried to escape".

"Stay still", he said, "and you will have a whole bag of money".

"I was very afraid and it still hurt me so much that I could do nothing. When everything was over, he gave me five pounds".

The confessions collected from these unfortunate young hired women hardly differed except in the price they were paid for their charms: ten pounds in the East End, twenty in the smarter West End. As for their recruitment, this was carried out by a well-known brothel-keeper who searched the provinces and brought back girls who had scarcely reached the age of puberty. In order to persuade them to follow him, he went around disguised as a clergyman and promised marriage to each one.

His confession is enlightening:

"After having courted her for a certain time", he said of one of his victims, "I pretended to get engaged to her; and to celebrate the event, I suggested taking her to London to see a comedy or a music-hall show. She was delighted at the idea and accepted my offer. I took her on a tour of places of amusement, then gave her something to eat, and especially a great deal to drink, with the result that she missed the last train. Meanwhile she was exhausted, fuddled with alcohol and bewildered by all the excitement of the evening; she was also terrifed to find herself alone in such a large town without any friends. I then gave her the address of comfortable lodgings for the night. My client took her virginity and I my ten or twenty pounds commission".

Men who bought the virginity of girls demanded that the fact that they were virgins should be proved and confirmed by a medical certificate, as was admitted to the "Gazette" reporters by the "Madame" of a house that was well-supplied with "undamaged goods":

"The three girls that I took to the doctors did not know each other at all. They were forbidden to speak amongst themselves or to hold hands. When we had gone into the doctor's the girls went in to see him one after the other, without making any remarks about it. Then, I gave them each five shillings for their trouble. I later received the following document, drawn up and initialled by the obliging doctor:

"London, 27th June 1885. By the present, I certify that I have examined D..., aged 16 years and have found her to be a virgin".

It was exactly the same for the others who, in their turn, signed the following agreement:

"By this document I consent to do what you wish in return for payment of the sum of 25 pounds, and to go to the place which you will indicate to me two days beforehand."

"Two of the three girls," went on the woman, "signed their names, the third, who was illiterate, simply made a cross. I must admit that I sold their virginity two or three times: to a priest, to a high official, to two diplomats and to three magistrates. Naturally none of them ever suspected that my little virgins were no longer intact..."

The results of the enquiry for the first time produced evidence to support what several historians and sexologists of the time had been claiming to be true, namely that "virgin hunting" had always been a hobby for the English.

PACISCOPI

In trying to discover the deeper origins of this attitude, one is tempted to see in it the individual intesification of a desire for power which was expressed elsewhere through colonial expansion, in Africa, and in the incredibly rapid progress of industrial development in Great Britain itself. Victorian England was still the England of Oliver Twist, Dickens' little orphan hero, whom poverty forced to work in a squalid workshop, where he was treated like a slave. The working conditions of children chained to their machines, often even in the literal sense of the word, were horrific. The threat of prostitution hung over girls, who were often snatched up in the country and drugged before being sold at a very low price. And since money and lack of any punishment encouraged perversion, those who indulged in it abandoned their proverbial phlegmatic nature to whip their partners in their sexual games until the blood flowed, or to deflower, with her consent or without it, some poor girl who was straight away afterwards thrown out into the street. Violence and blood were, for them, inseparable from the domination of the flesh. But virginity was for them also a guarantee against the risk of catching venereal diseases.

The secret system that the "Pall Mall Gazette" brought to light depended on the protection that the police granted to procurers in return from sums which were sometimes as large as 500 pounds a year. There was an enormous scandal. The Archbishop of Canterbury lost no sleep over it, however, nor the Salvation Army, nor the "White Ribbon", nor even the "Ladies of Pimlico"... A few minor offenders were arrested, but the traffic continued; and the prices rose. As for the "Pall Mall Gazette", it simply earned for itself the reputation of being an obscene newspaper.

Queen Victoria died, and was succeeded by her son, the lively Edward VII, who celebrated at Montmartre and Pigalle. In one of the brothels of which he was a regular customer, he was provided with a chair made specially for him, "The Recalcitrant's Armchair", so called "because it allowed him to obtain by force, used even to a moderate extent, what would have been refused to him by the use of gentleness". One of his occasional partners mentions "the difficult positions" but admits nevertheless that for the price he paid "it was worth it".

Queen Victoria would turn in her grave if she could hear such remarks, and with her a large number of her prudish contemporaries now passed away; too soon perhaps for them to have been able in their turn to yield to the temptations of Eros; with a feeling as much of regret as of repentance...

94